I0488668

How To Draw Realistic Skulls Volume 4

Simple Guide to Drawing Skulls

How to Draw Skulls

By : Gala Publication

2

Published By :

Gala Publication

© Copyright 2015 – Gala Publication

ISBN-13: **978-1522785873**
ISBN-10: **1522785876**

Table of Contents

CASSETTE SKULL

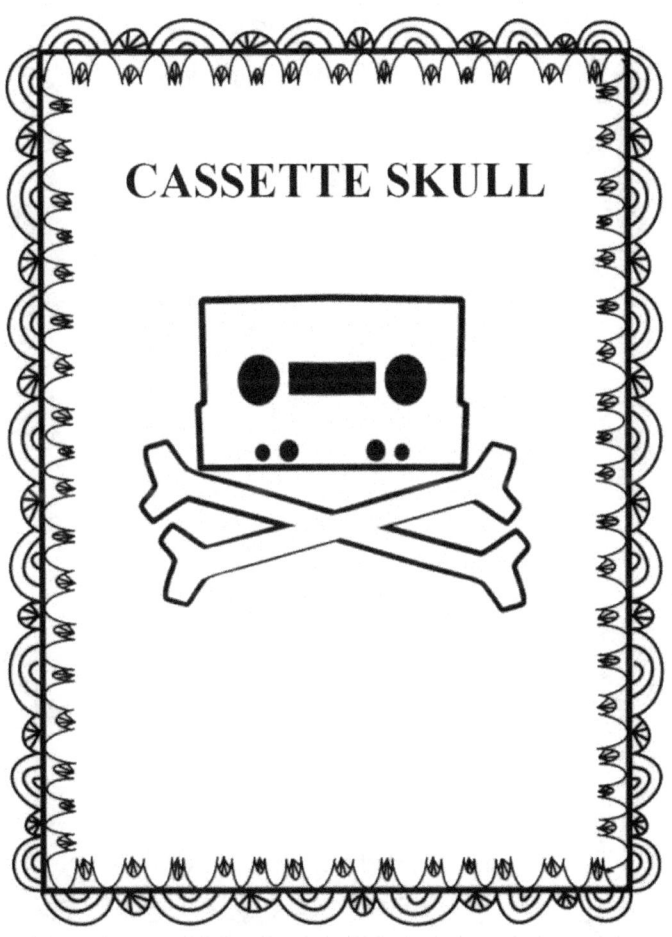

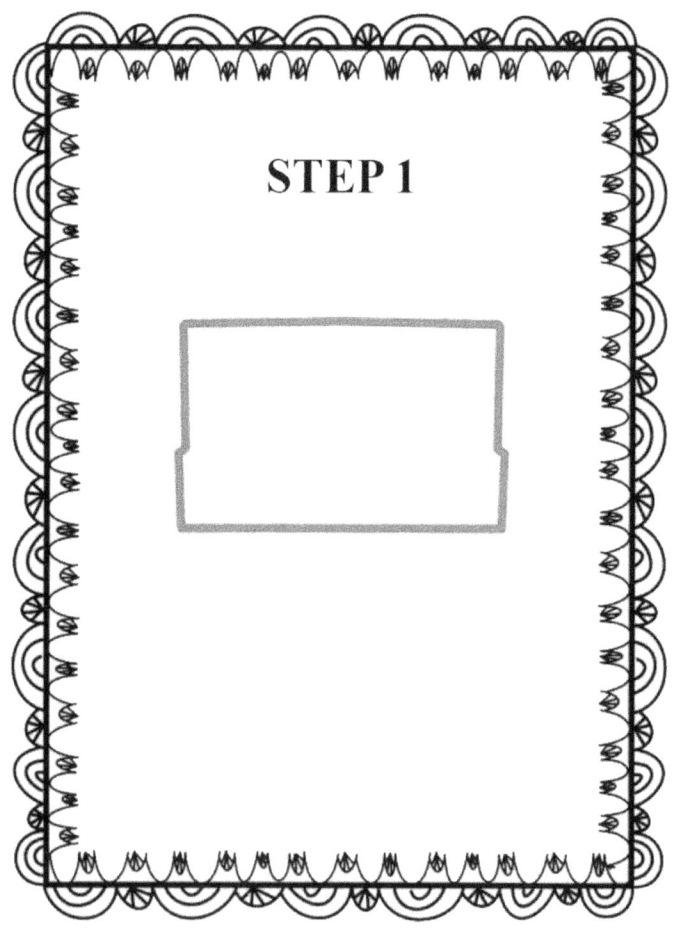

STEP 1

STEP 2

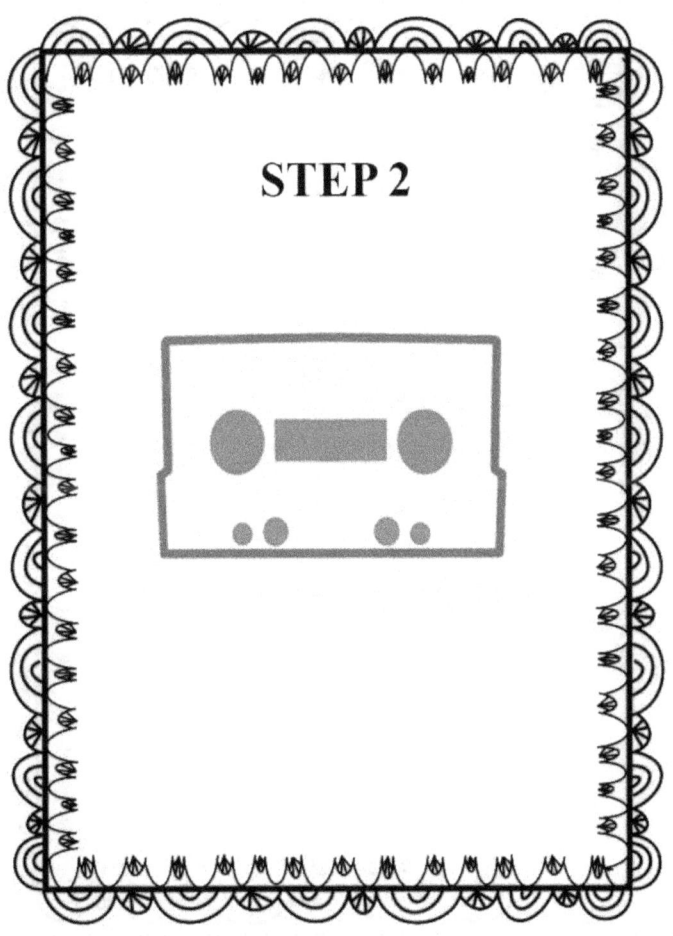

STEP 3

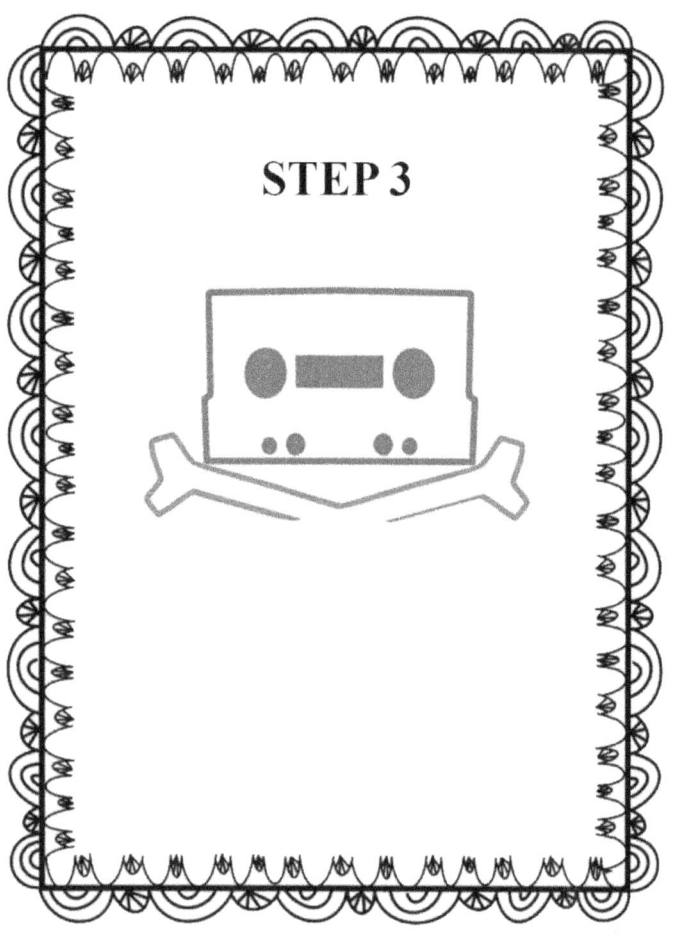

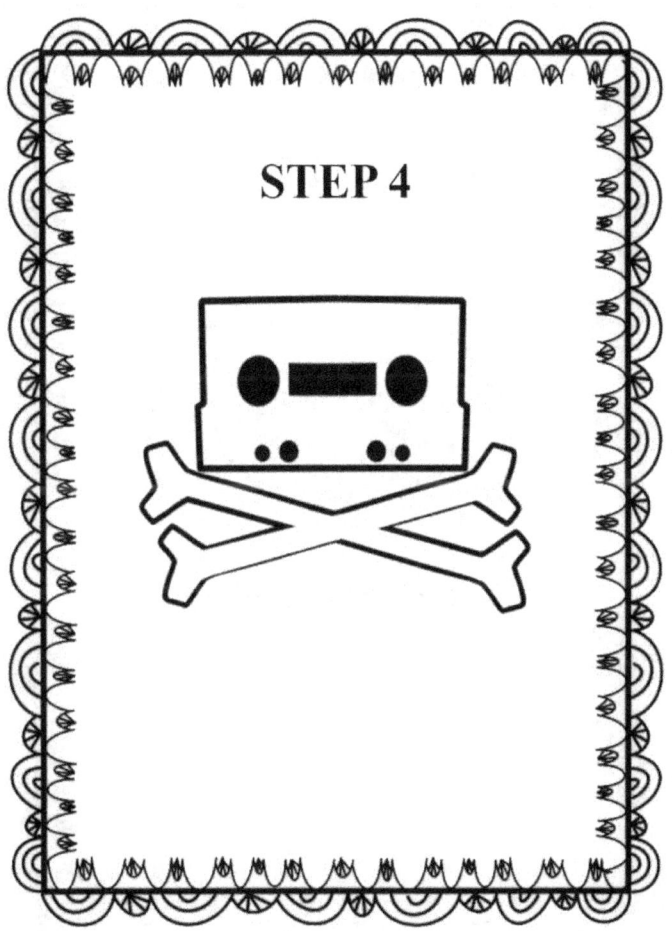

STEP 4

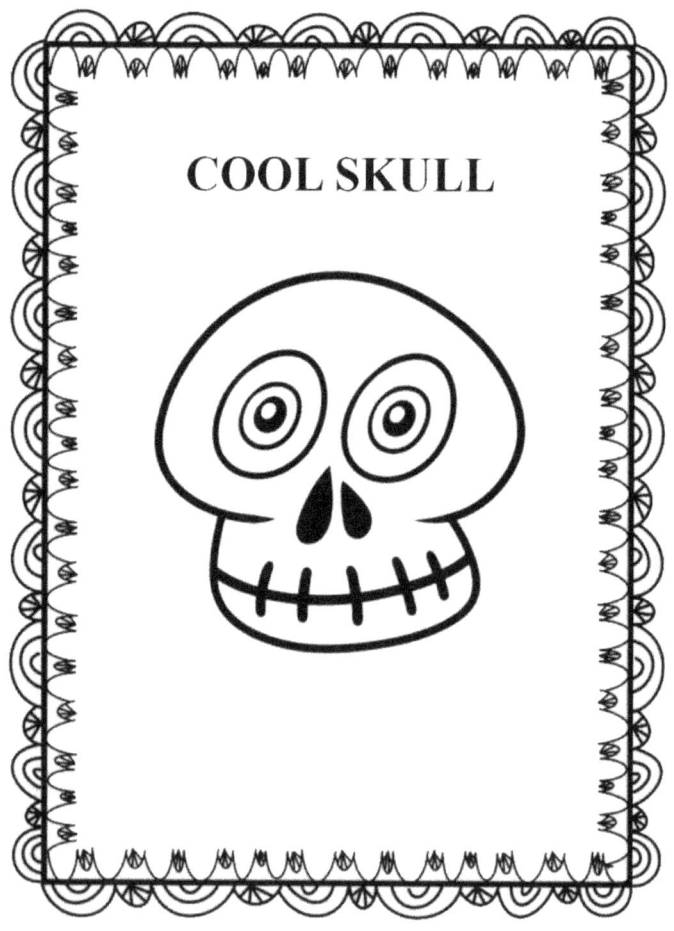

STEP 1

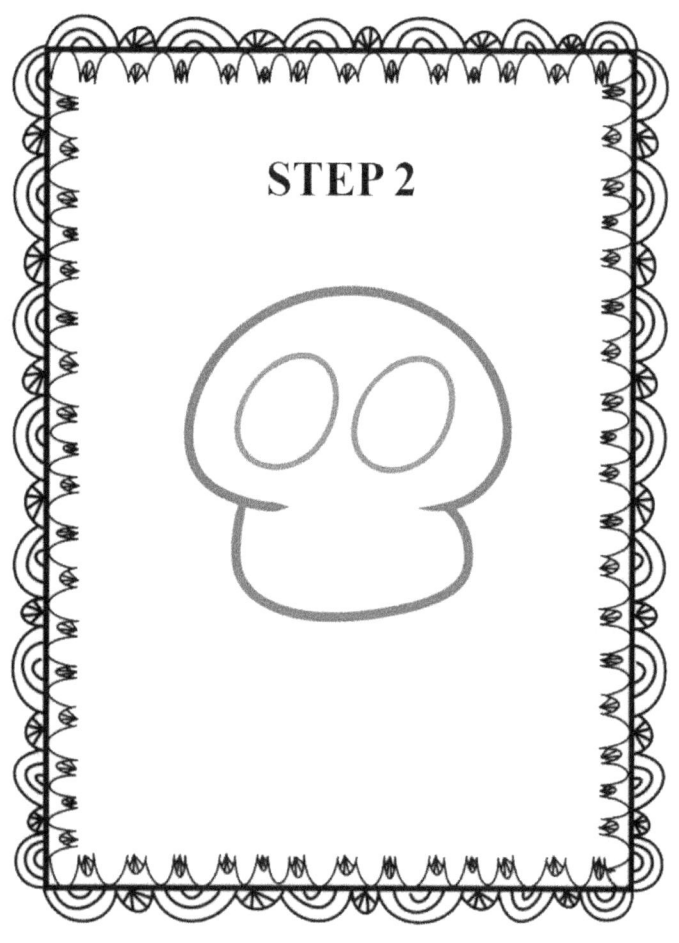

STEP 3

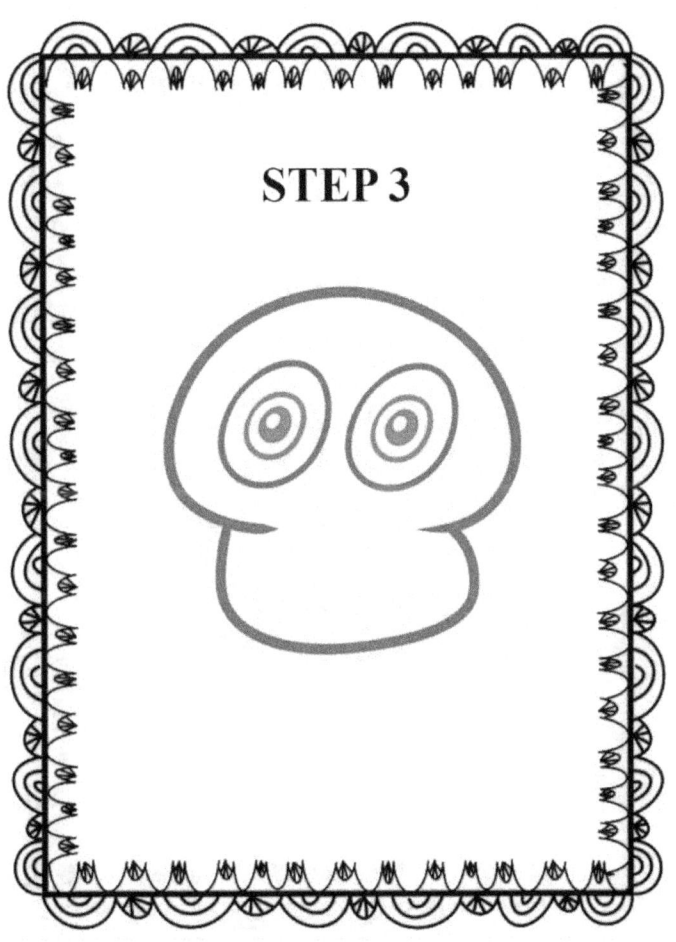

STEP 4

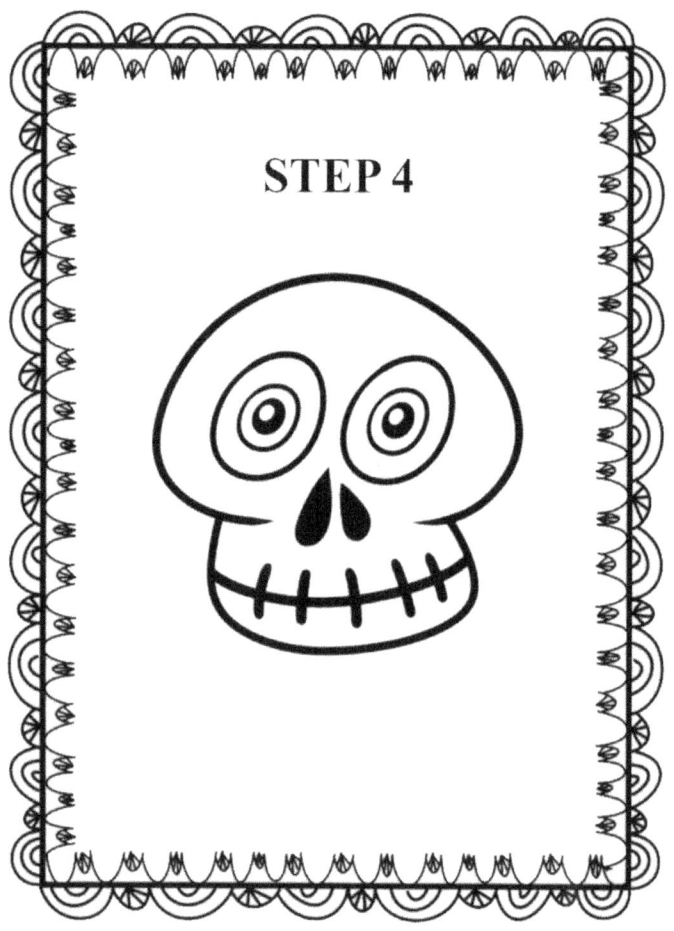

GENTLEMAN SKULL

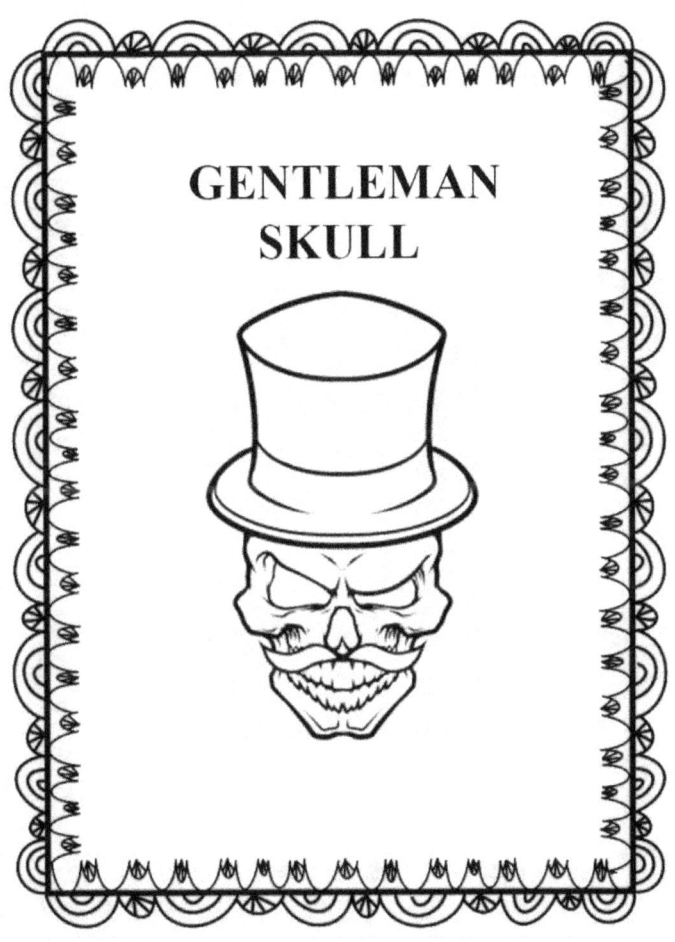

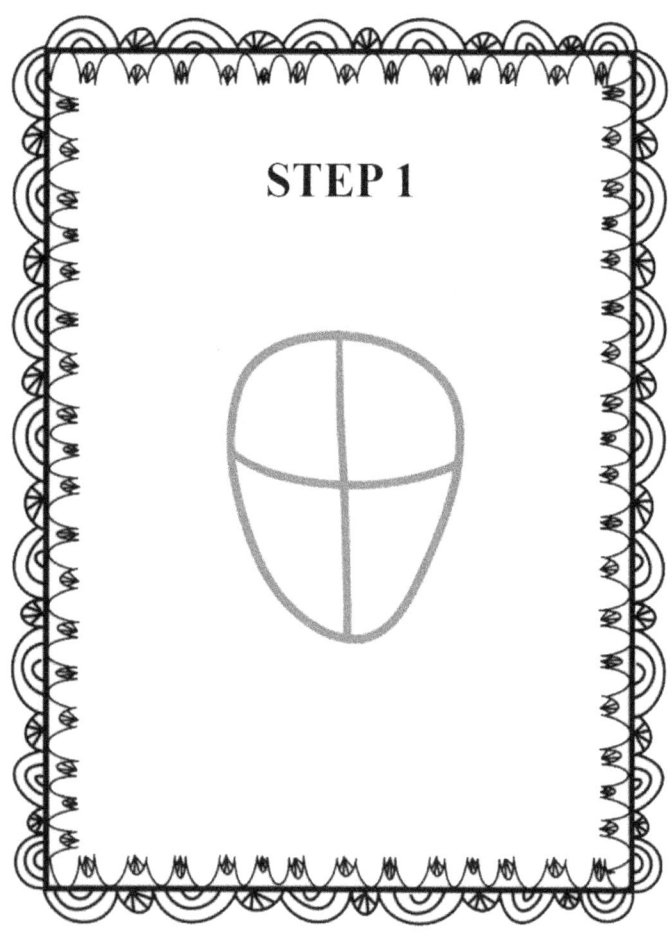

STEP 1

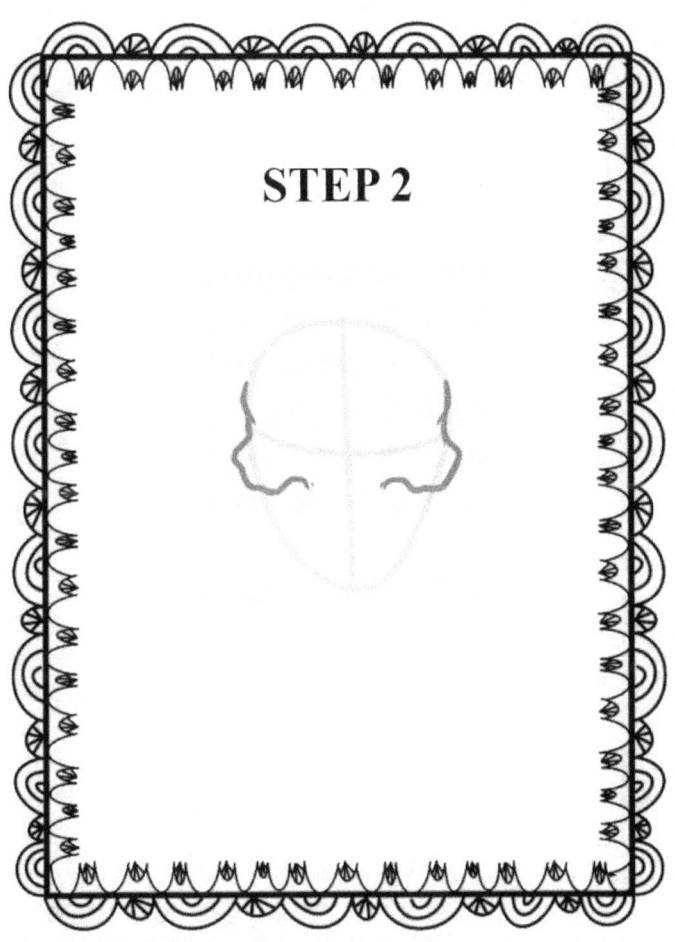

STEP 2

STEP 3

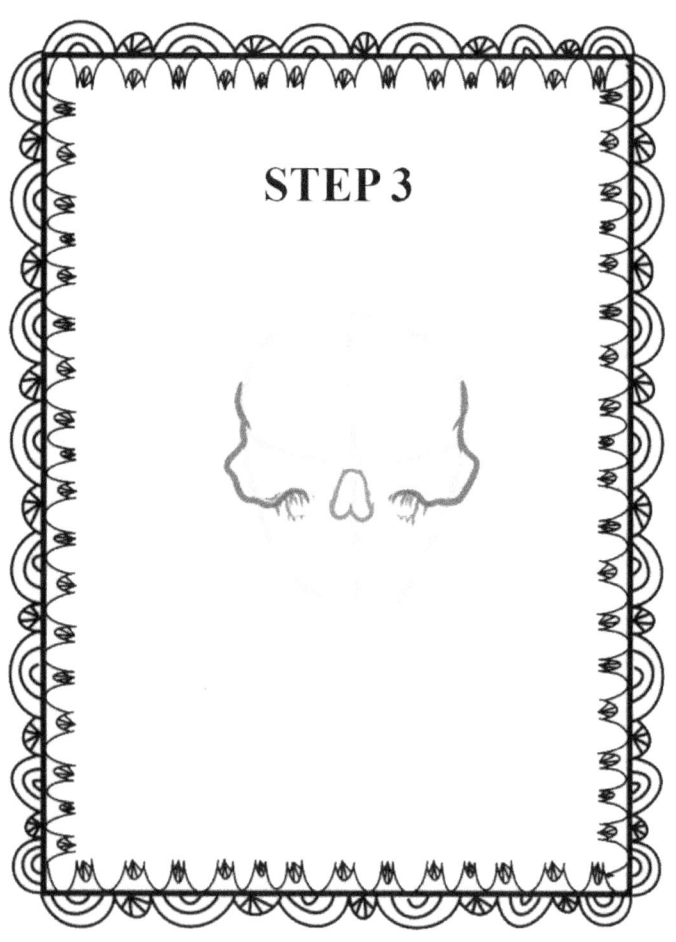

STEP 4

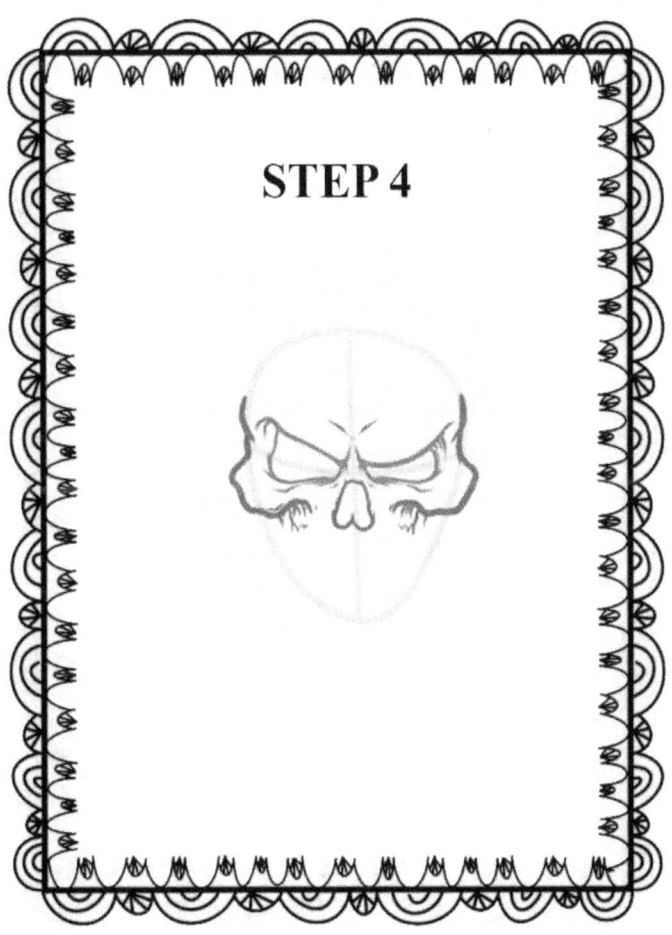

STEP 5

STEP 6

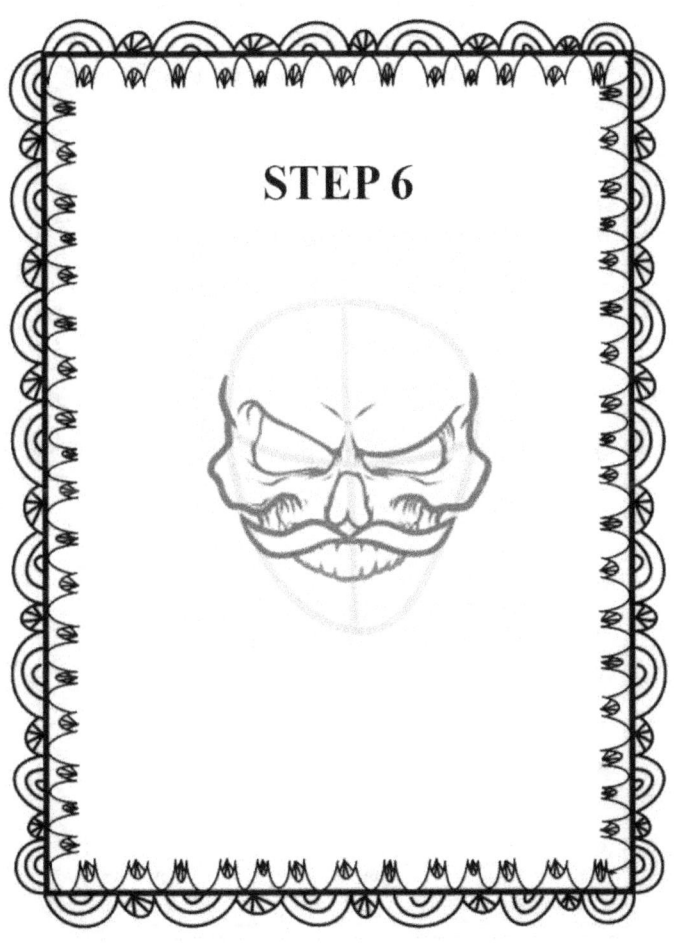

STEP 7

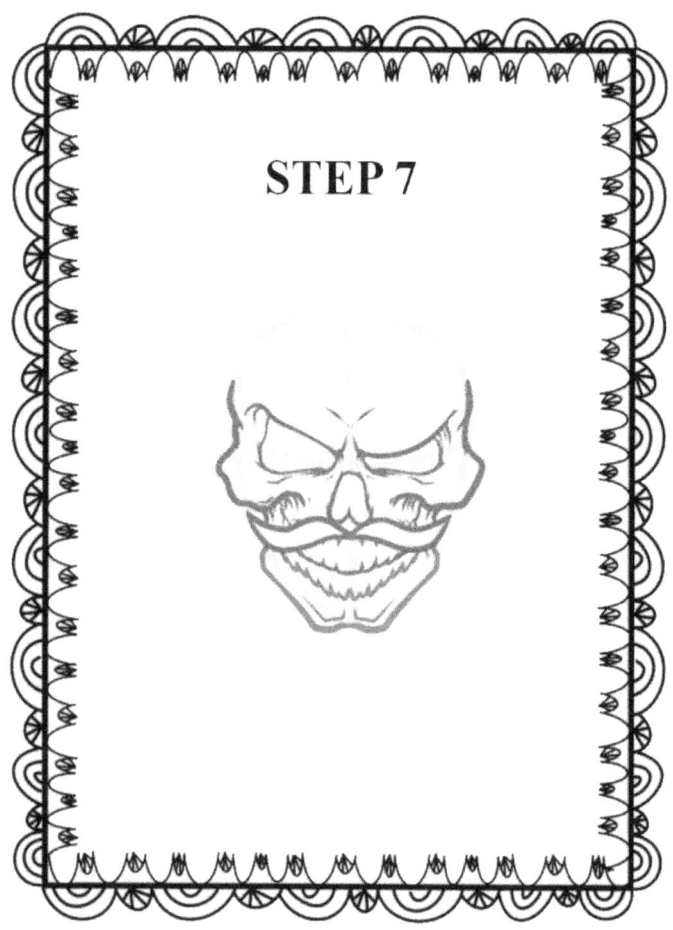

STEP 8

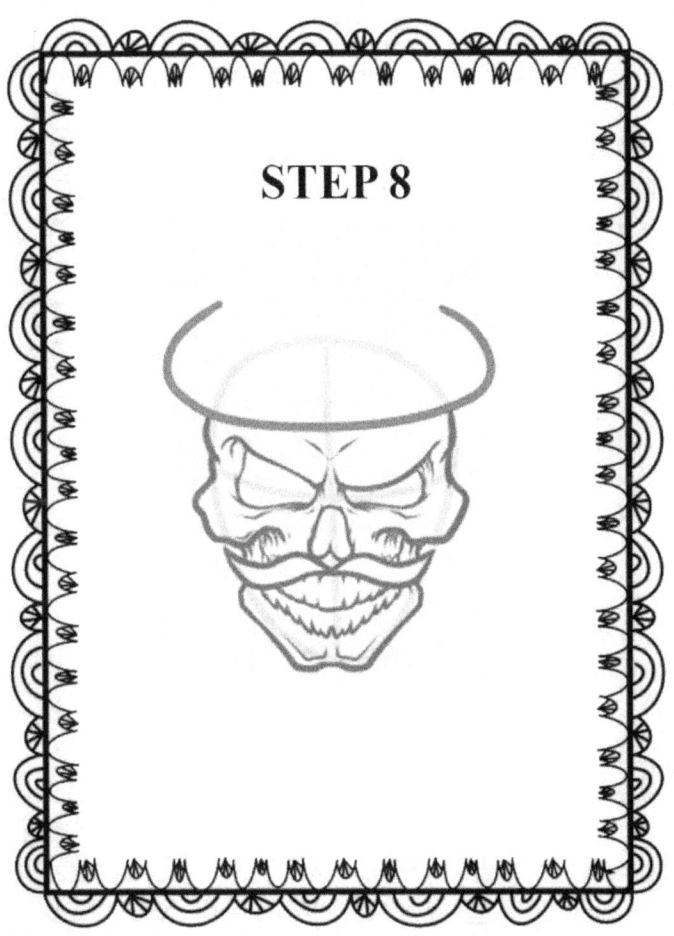

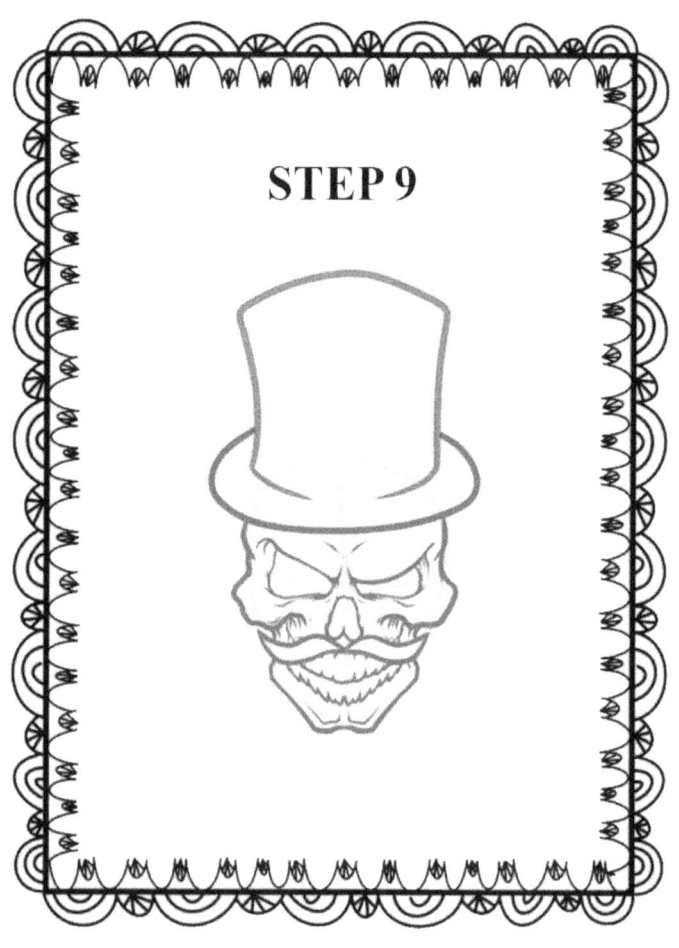

STEP 10

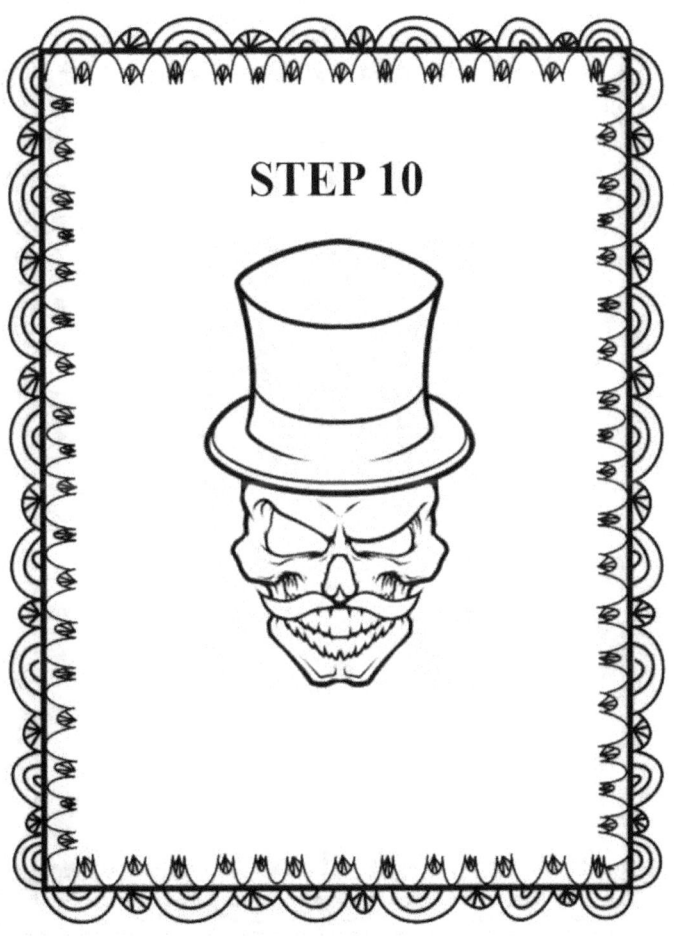

SAM SKULL

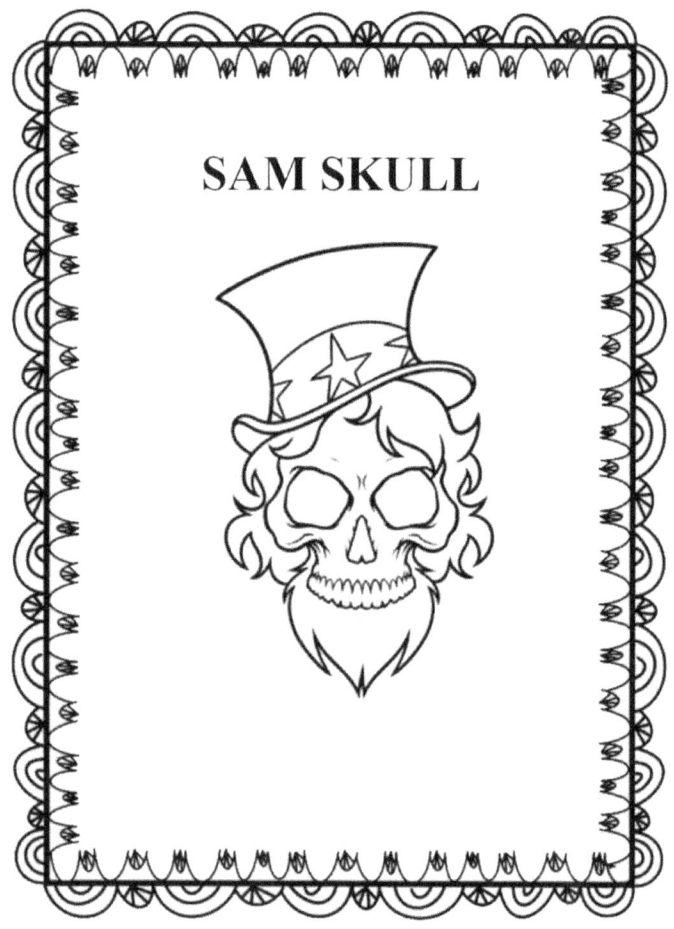

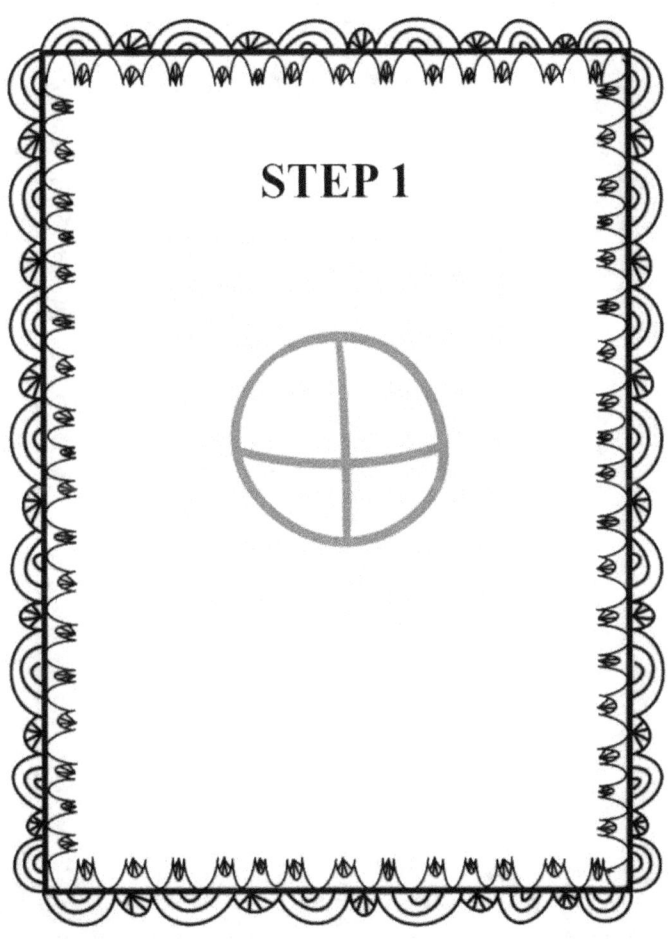

STEP 1

STEP 2

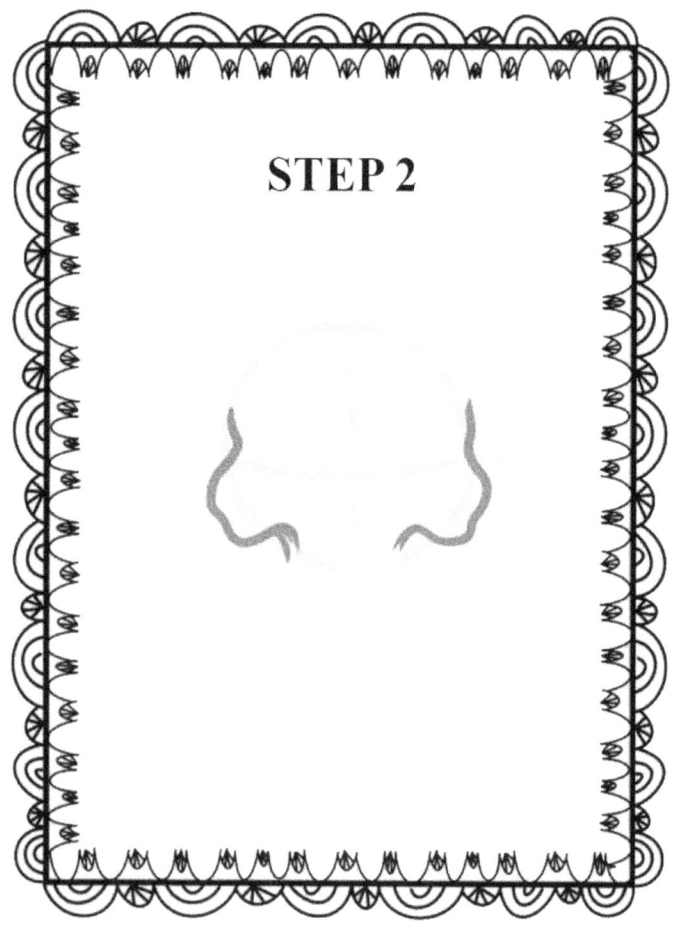

STEP 3

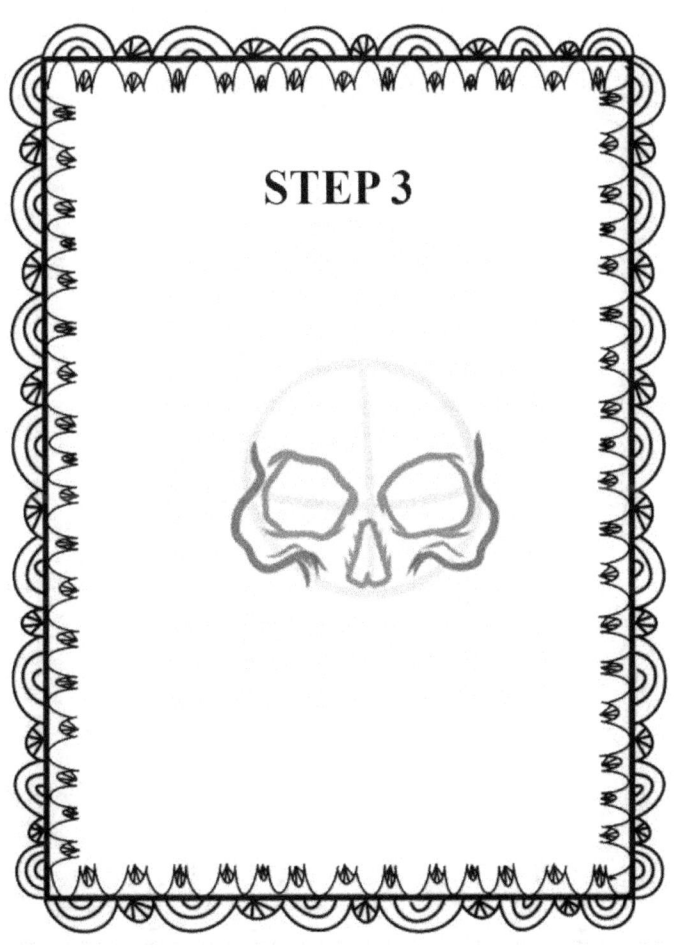

STEP 4

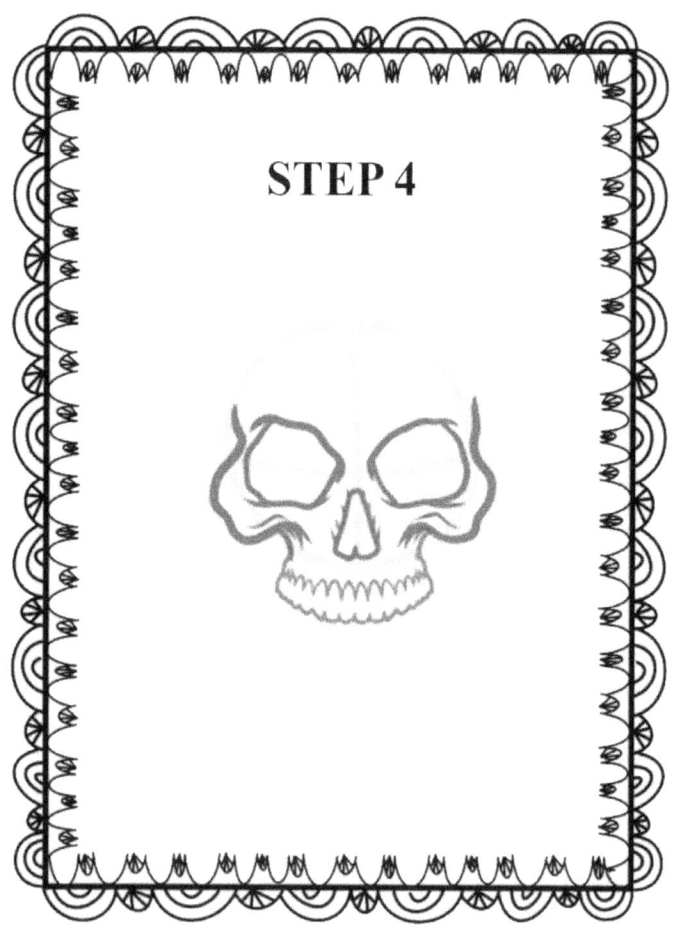

STEP 5

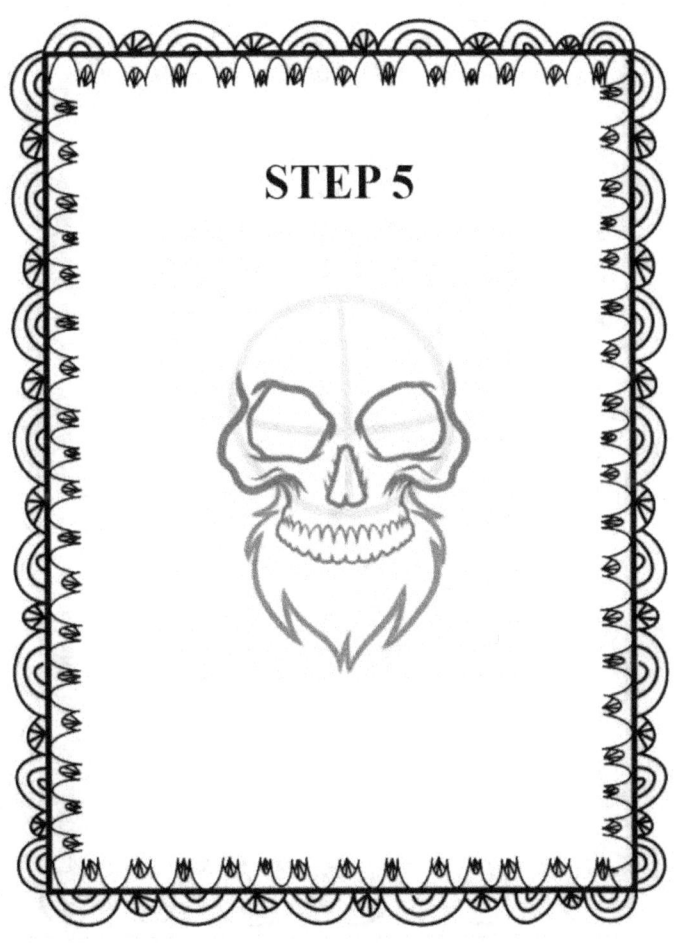

STEP 6

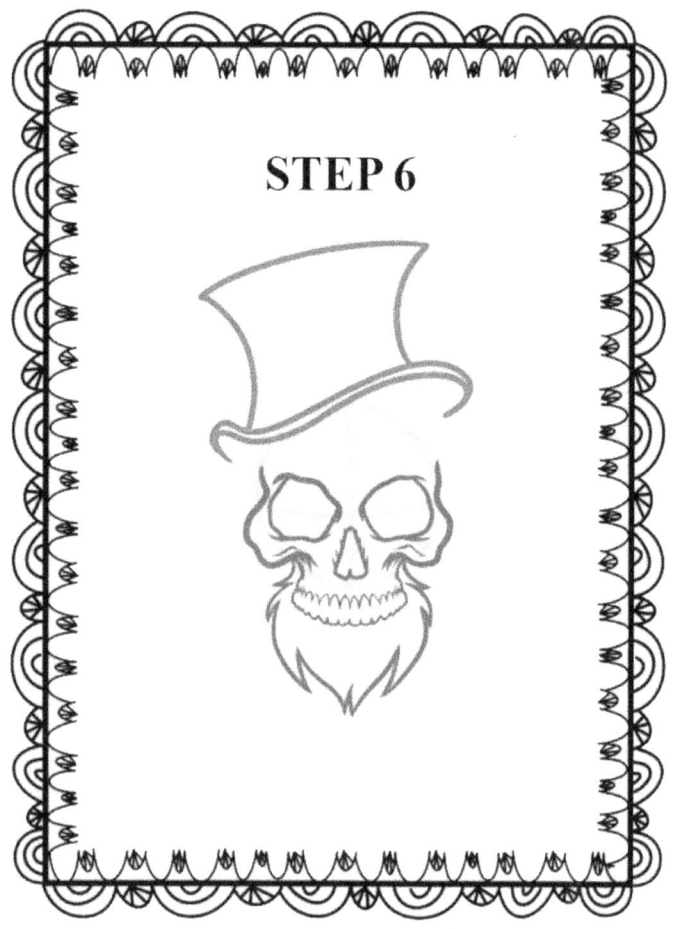

STEP 7

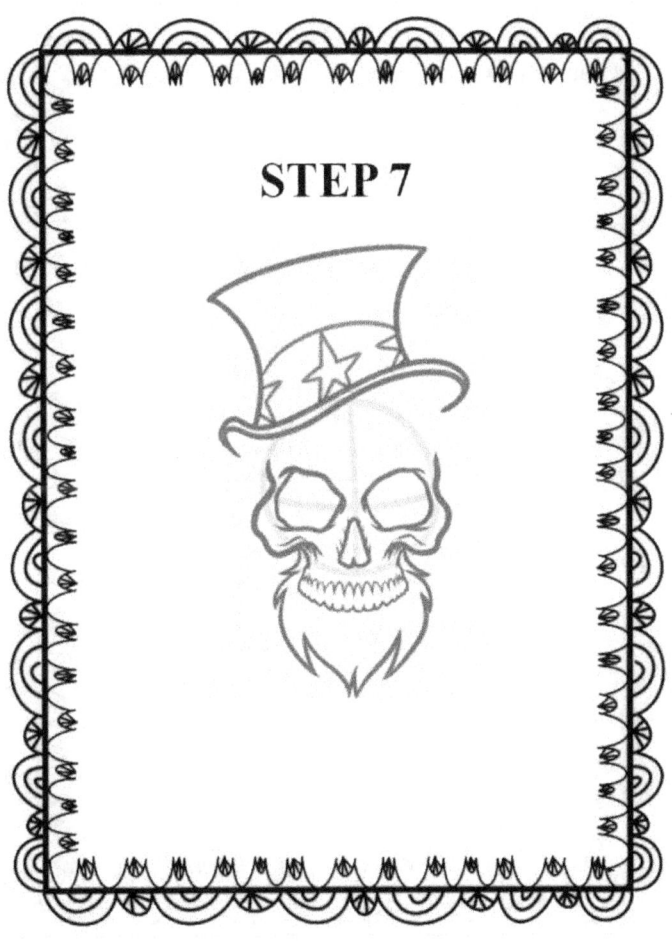

STEP 8

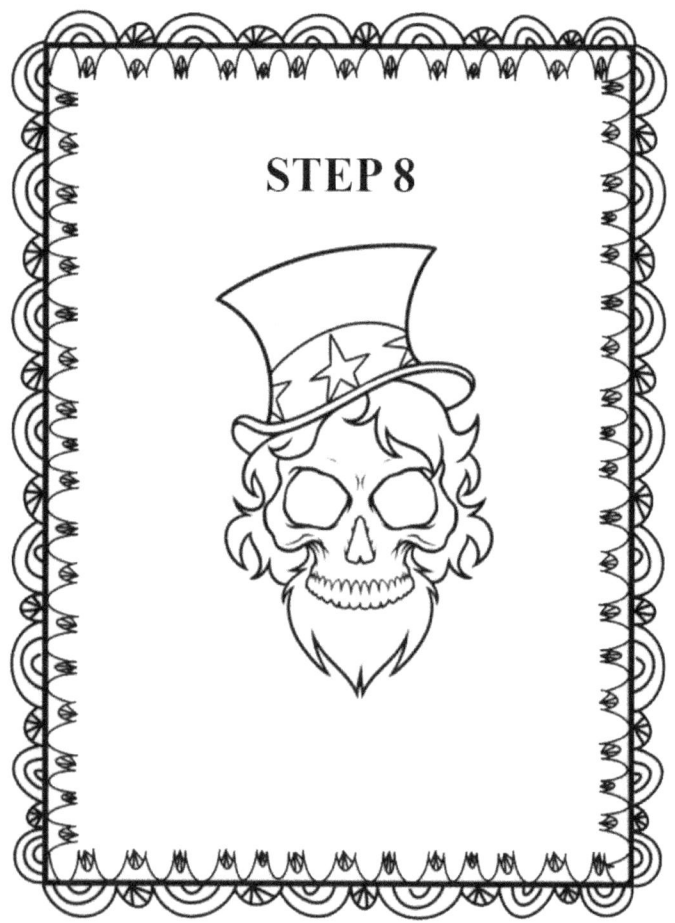

SPIDER SKULL

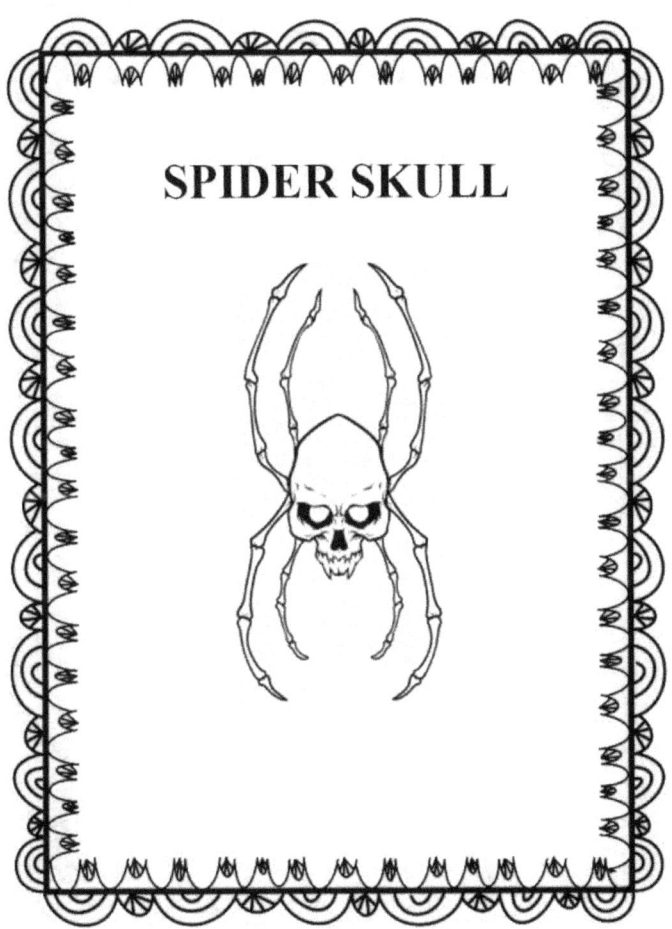

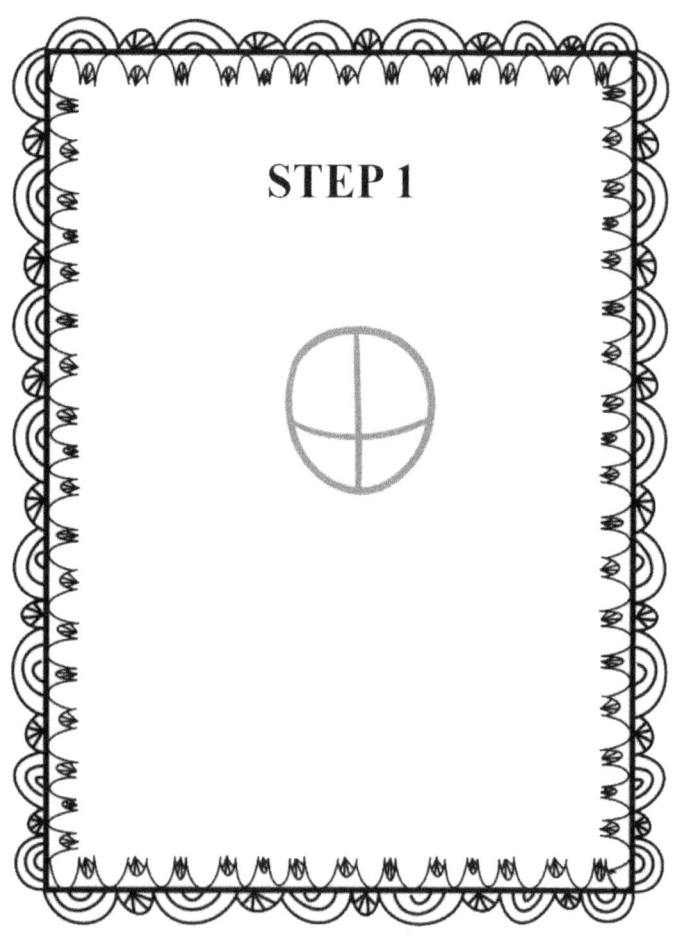

STEP 2

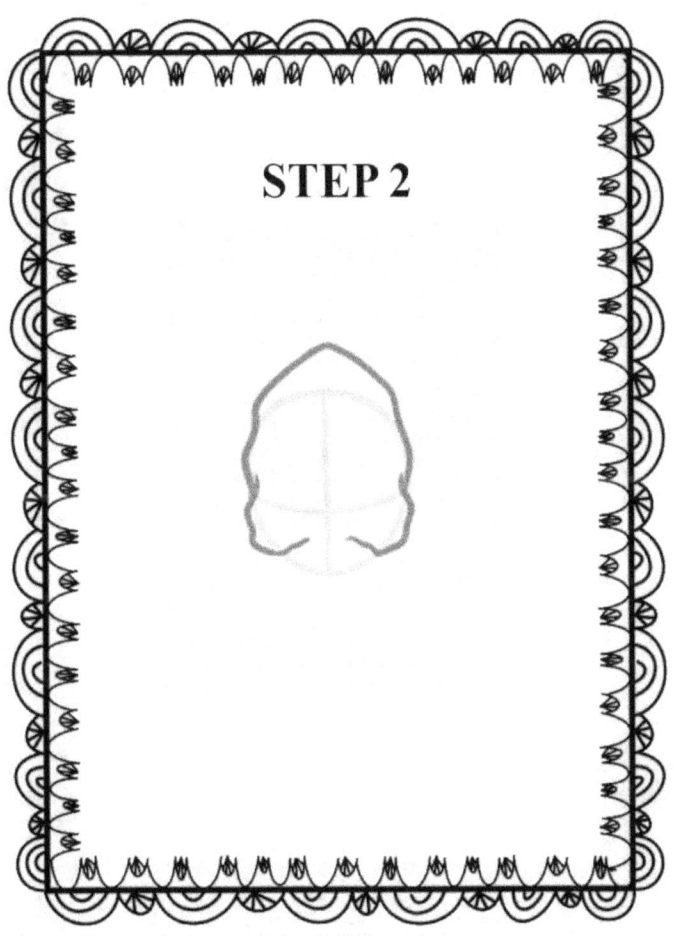

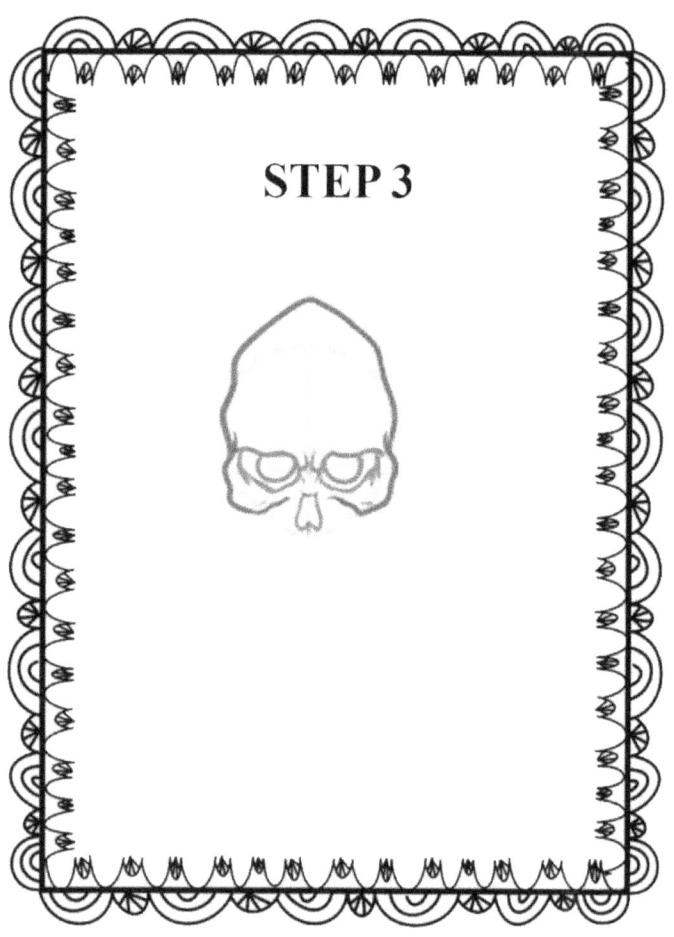

STEP 3

STEP 4

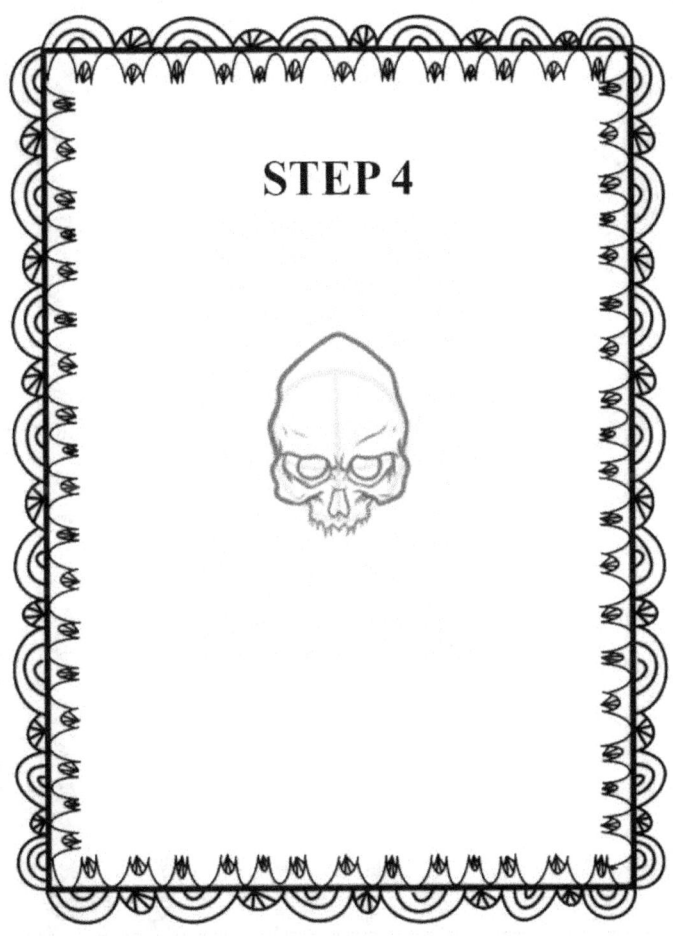

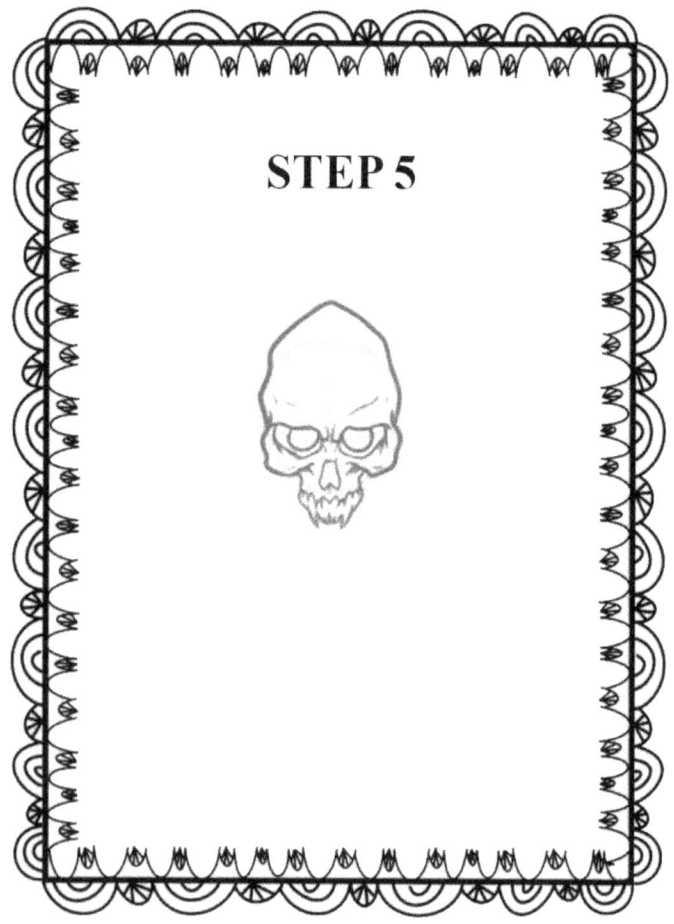

STEP 5

STEP 6

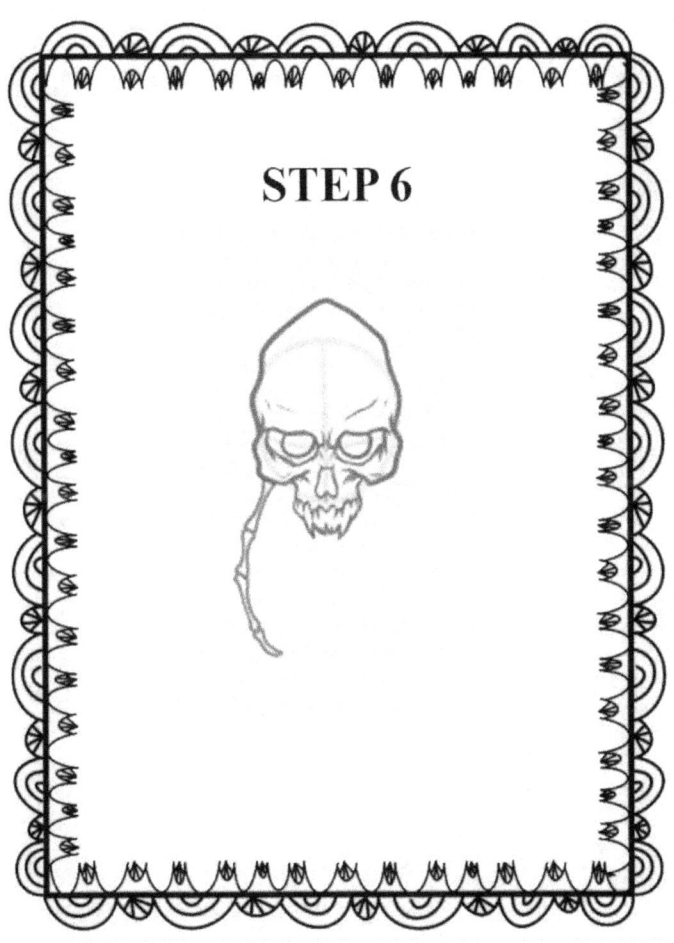

STEP 7

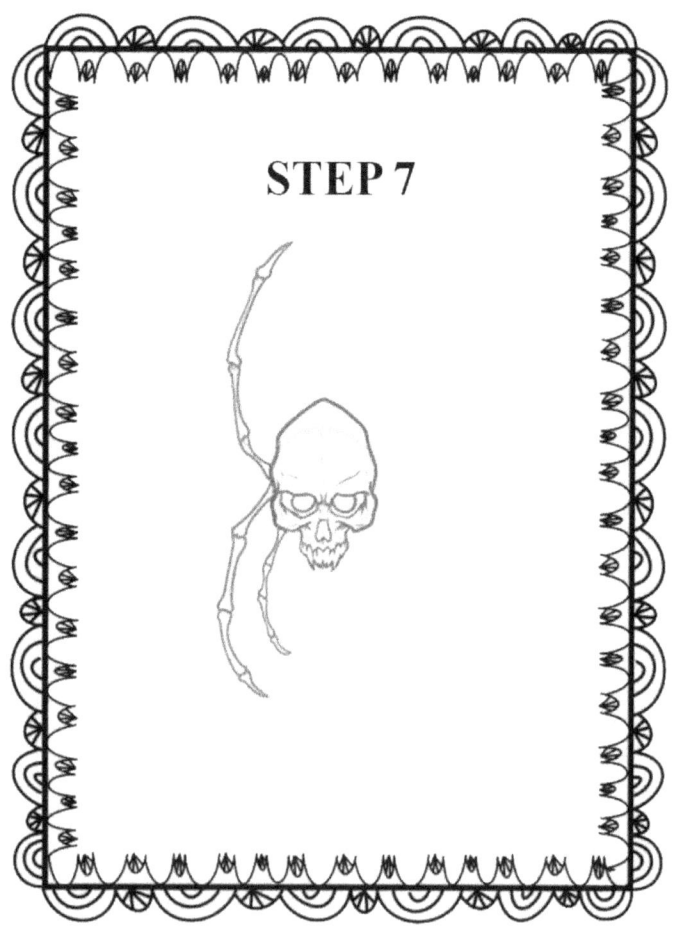

43

STEP 8

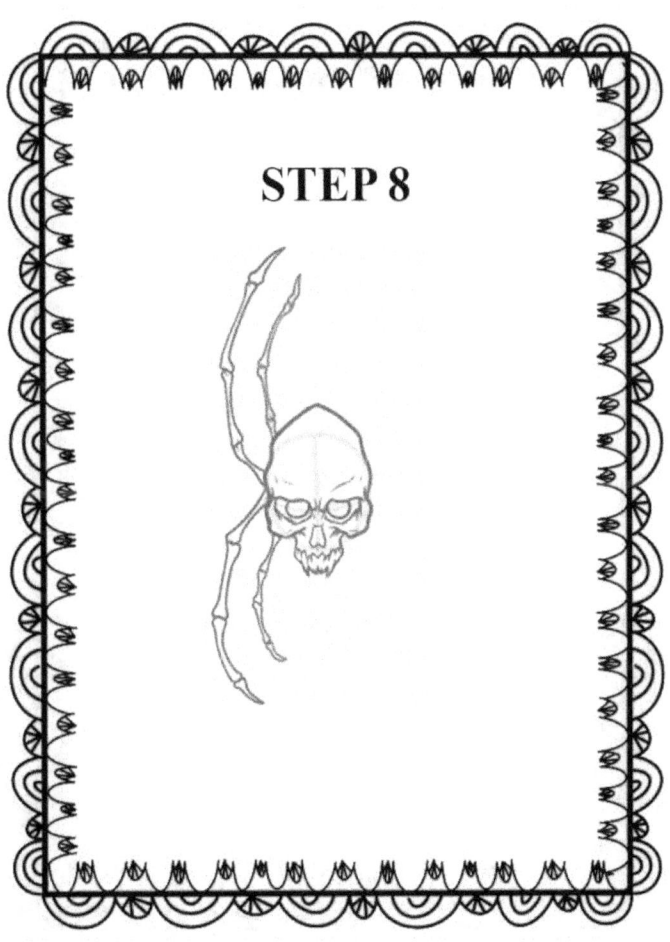

STEP 9

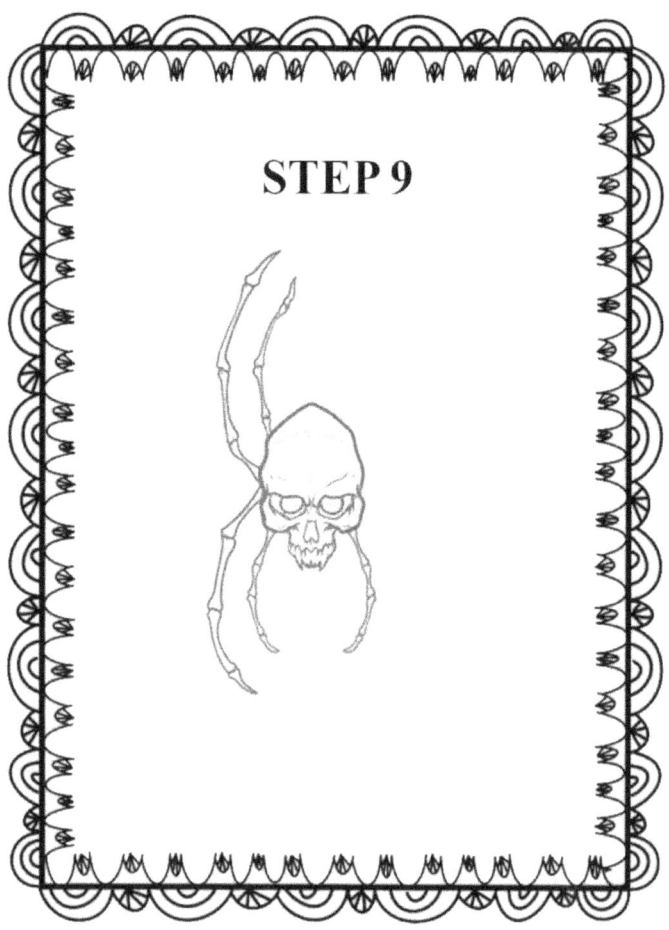

STEP 10

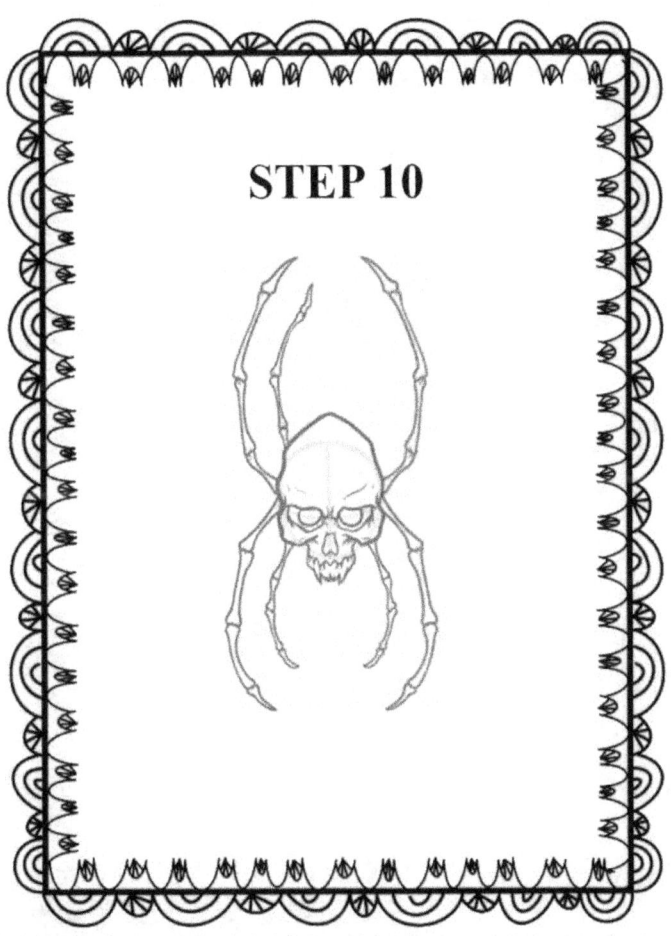

STEP 11

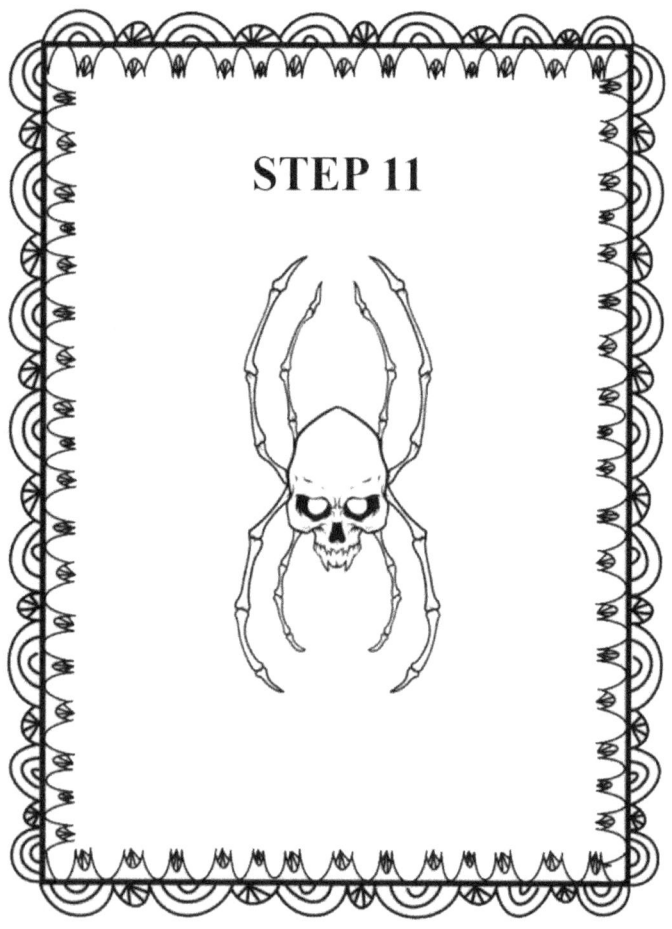

TRIPPY SKULL

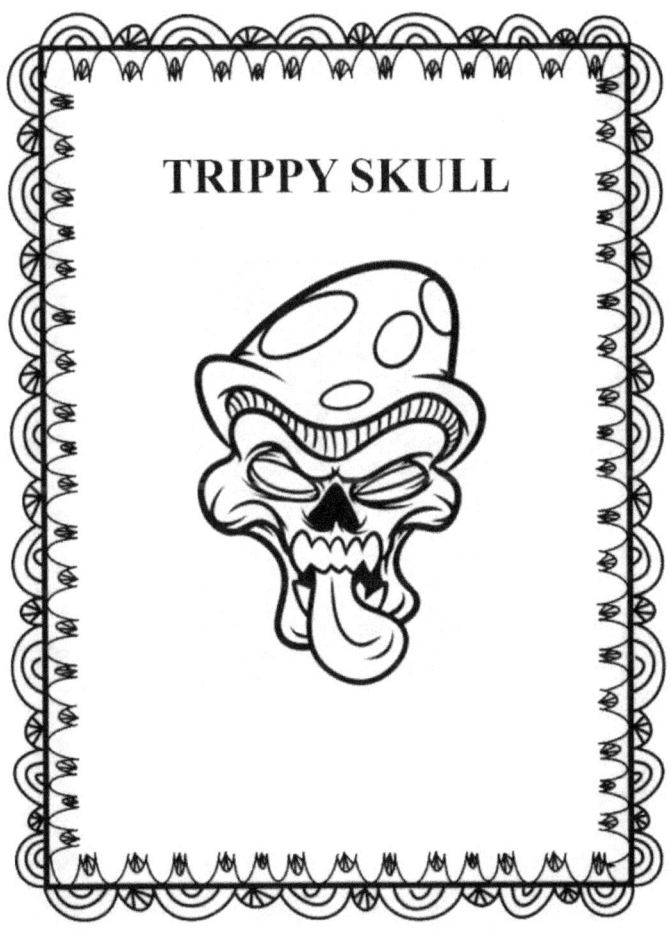

49

STEP 2

STEP 3

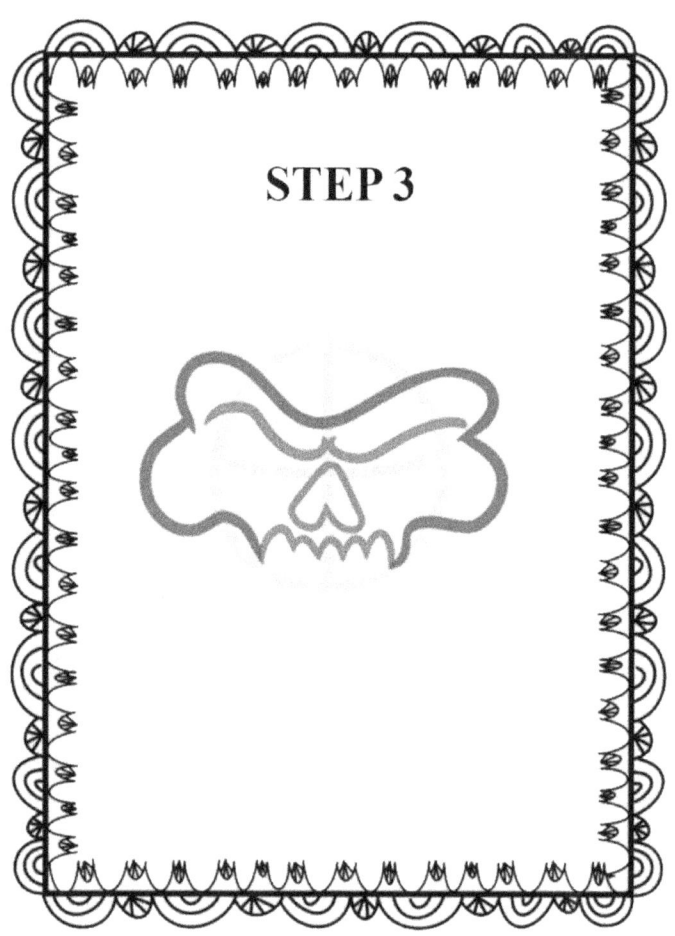

STEP 4

STEP 5

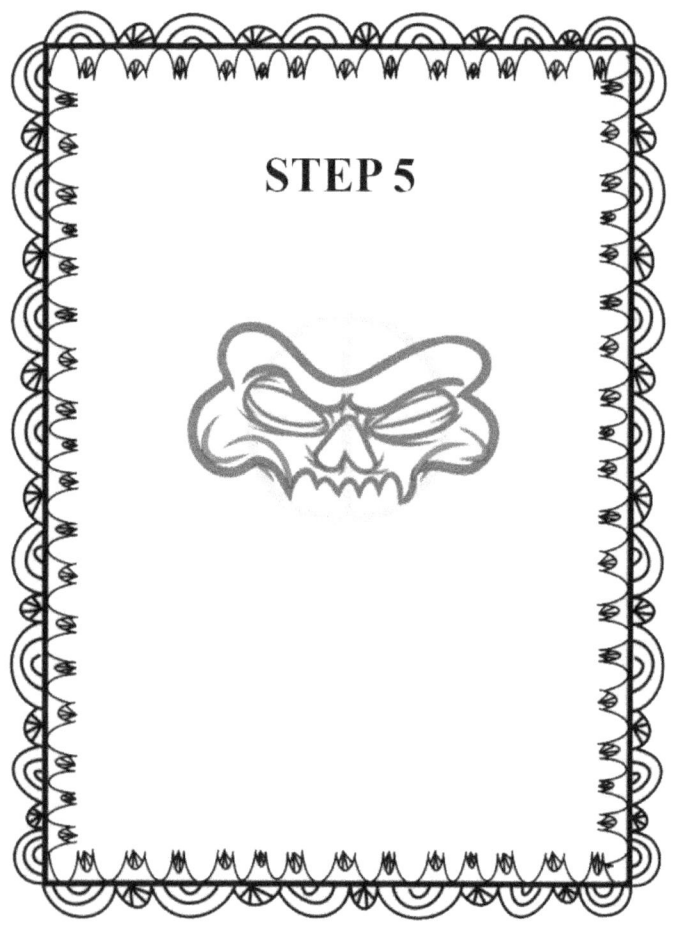

STEP 6

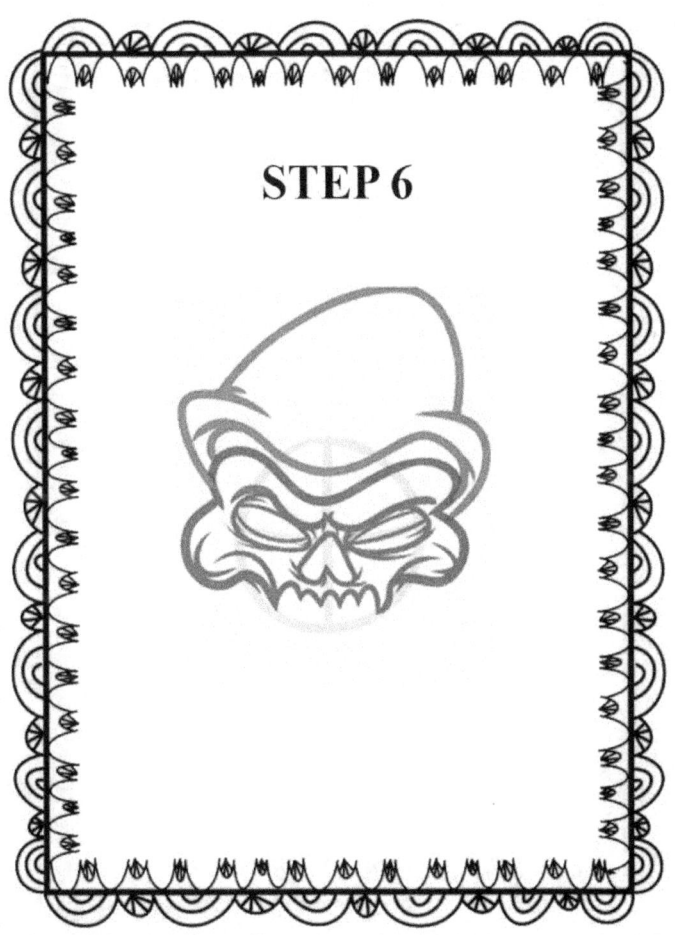

STEP 7

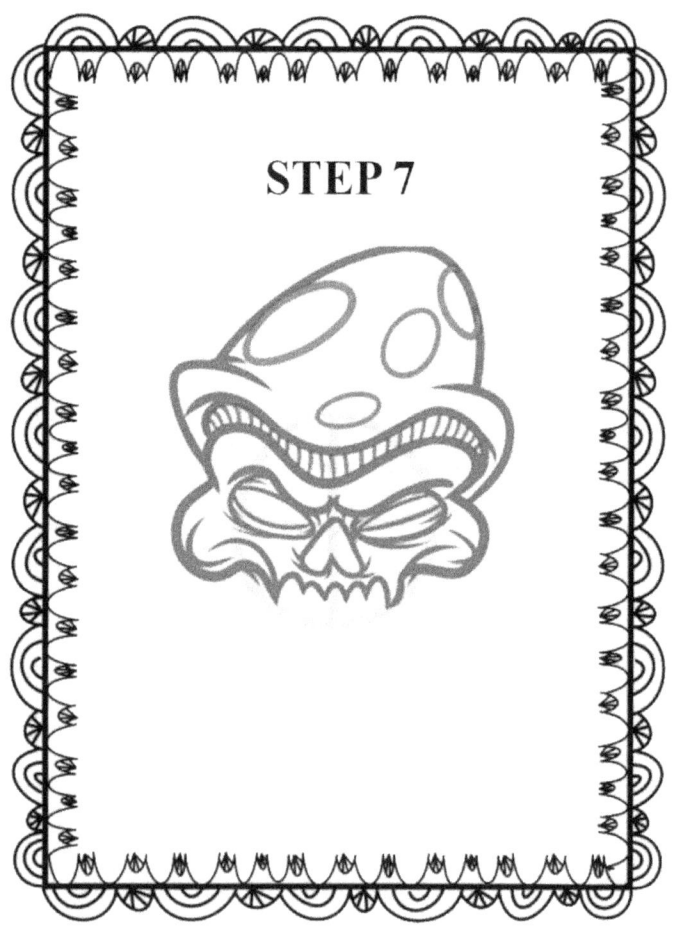

STEP 8

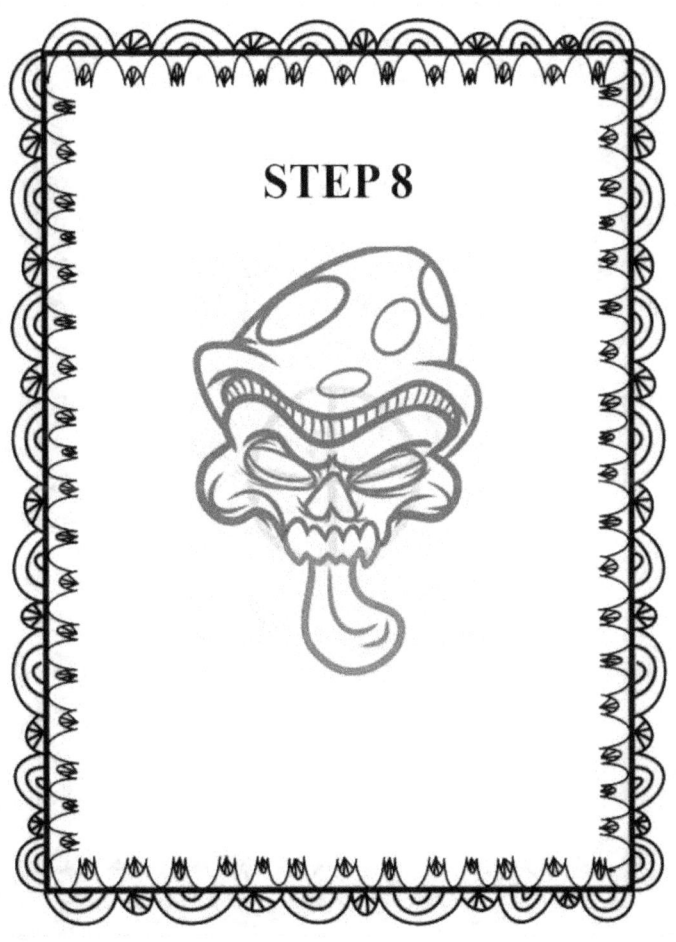

STEP 9

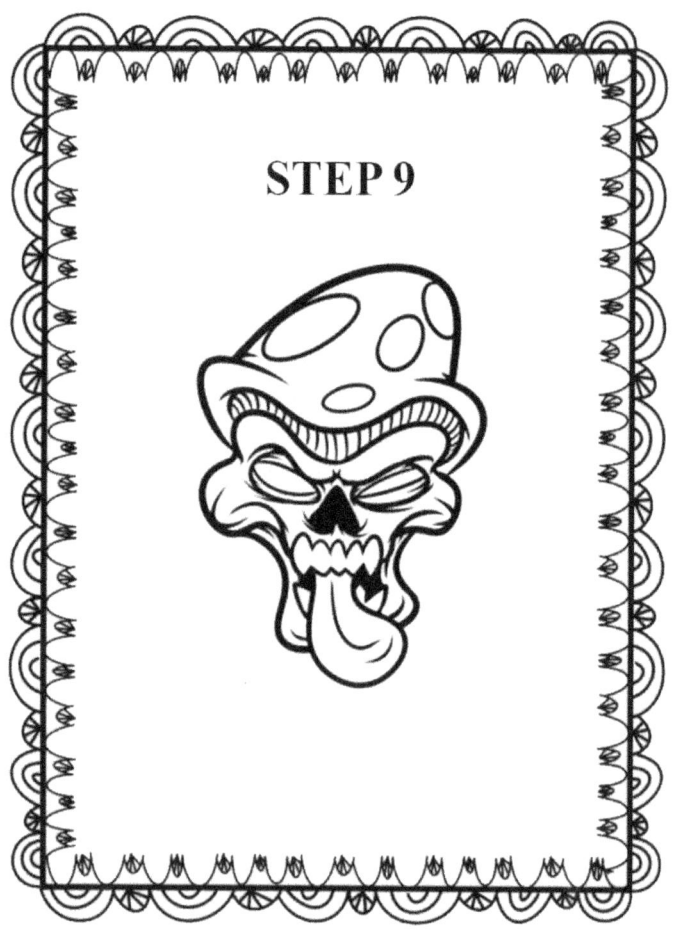